take it apart

TRAIN

By Chris Oxlade

Illustrated by Mike Grey

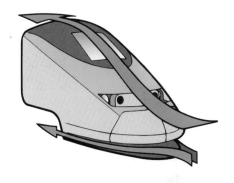
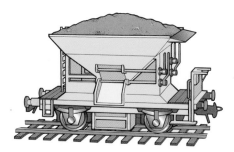
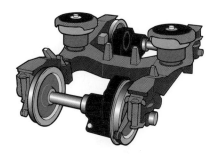

Thameside Press

US publication copyright © 2002 Thameside Press.
International copyright reserved in all countries.
No part of this book may be reproduced in any form
without written permission from the publisher.

Distributed in the United States by
Smart Apple Media
1980 Lookout Drive
North Mankato, MN 56003

Text copyright © Chris Oxlade
Illustrator copyright © Mike Grey

ISBN 1-930643-96-9

Library of Congress Control Number 2002 141350

Editor: Veronica Ross
Designer: Guy Callaby
Illustrator: Mike Grey
Researcher: Susie Brooks
Consultants: Elizabeth Atkinson and Robin Kerrod

Printed by South China Printing Co. Ltd., Hong Kong

Inside This Book

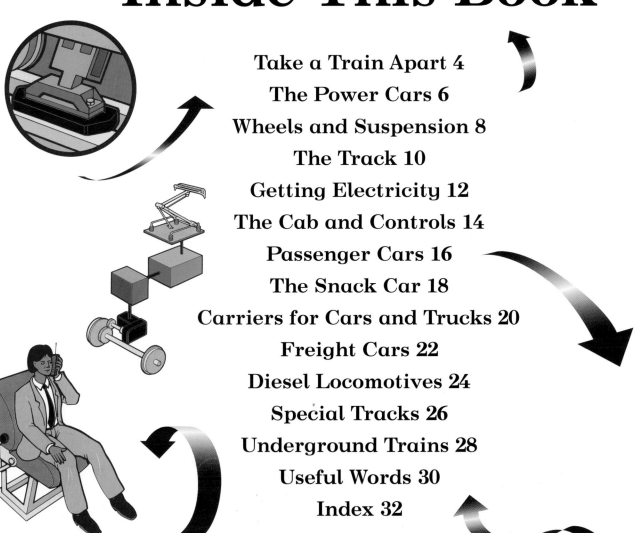

Take a Train Apart

🔩 **A train is made of thousands of parts. Some parts are very tiny. Some parts are big and heavy.**

🔩 **The parts are made from metal, plastic, rubber, glass, and many other materials.**

🔩 **This book shows you the main parts of an electric express train.**

Fact Box
The fastest passenger train in the world is a French electric express train called the TGV. It speeds along at up to 186 miles per hour.

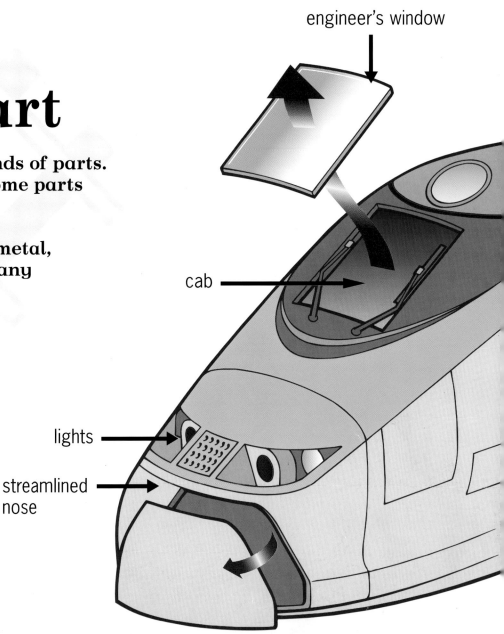

engineer's window

cab

lights

streamlined nose

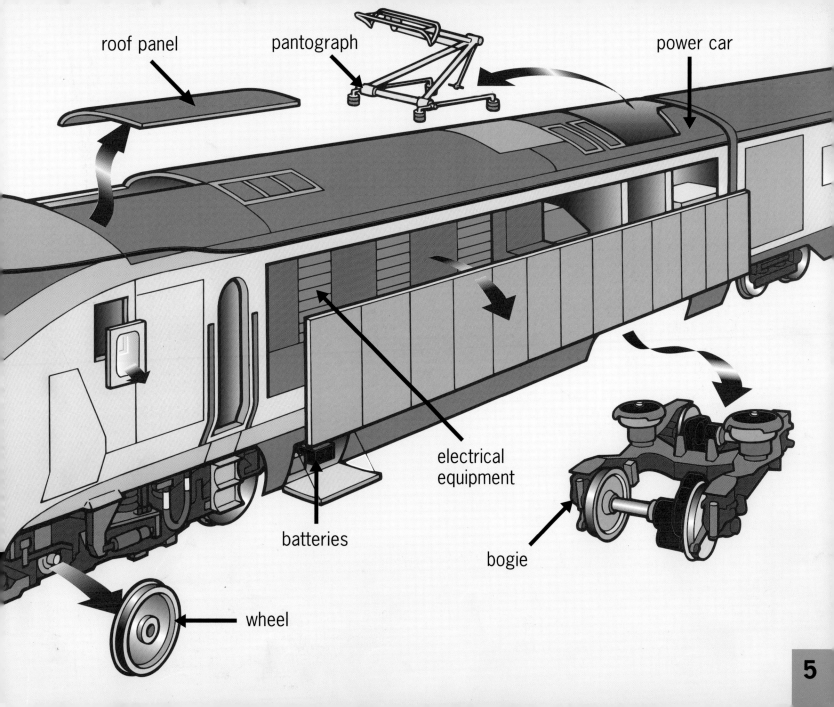

roof panel

pantograph

power car

electrical
equipment

batteries

bogie

wheel

5

The Power Cars

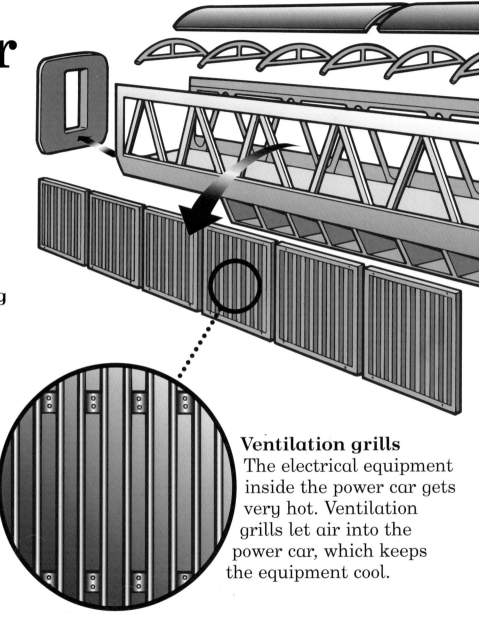

- There is a power car at each end of the train.

- The machinery inside makes the train move along.

- Each power car has a strong frame covered in thin panels.

- At the front is a cab for the train engineer.

Fact Box
Some trains have special power cars and passenger cars that lean over to the side when the train speeds around curves.

Ventilation grills
The electrical equipment inside the power car gets very hot. Ventilation grills let air into the power car, which keeps the equipment cool.

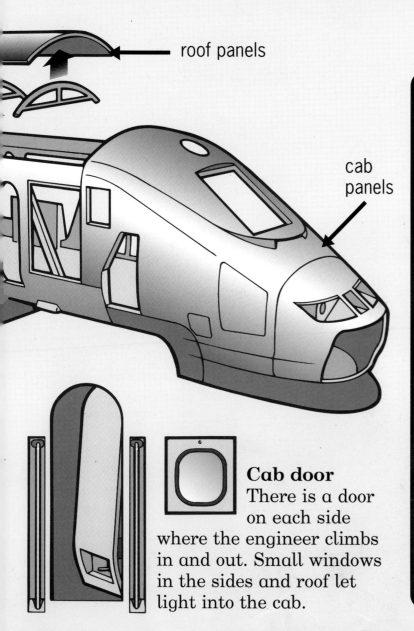

roof panels

cab panels

Cab door
There is a door on each side where the engineer climbs in and out. Small windows in the sides and roof let light into the cab.

Air flow

When you run or ride a bike, you feel wind in your face. This is the air pushing against you. The faster you go, the more you have to push against the air. The front of an express train is rounded and smooth so that the air flows around it easily and does not slow down the train too much. This is called streamlining.

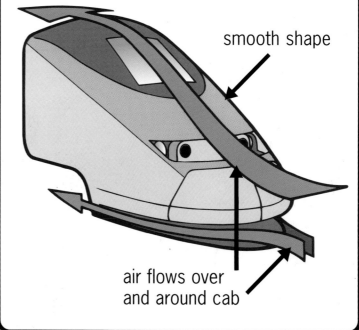

smooth shape

air flows over and around cab

Wheels and Suspension

⚙ The train's wheels are in sets of four. They are attached to a frame called a bogie.

⚙ There is a bogie at both ends of the power cars and other train cars. The bogies swivel from side to side.

⚙ Each wheel has a spring, which gives a comfortable ride over small bumps in the track.

Fact Box
The biggest type of steam locomotive ever built was the American *Big Boy*. Each locomotive had 24 wheels and weighed 595 tons.

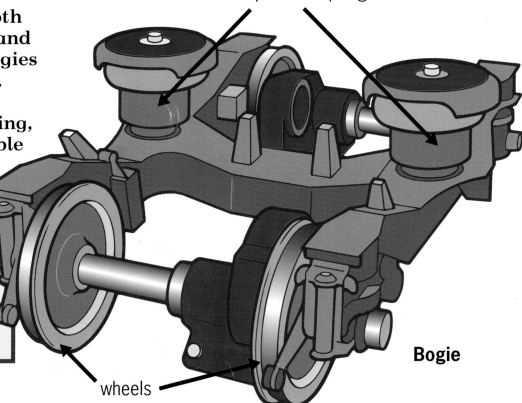

axle

suspension springs

wheels

Bogie

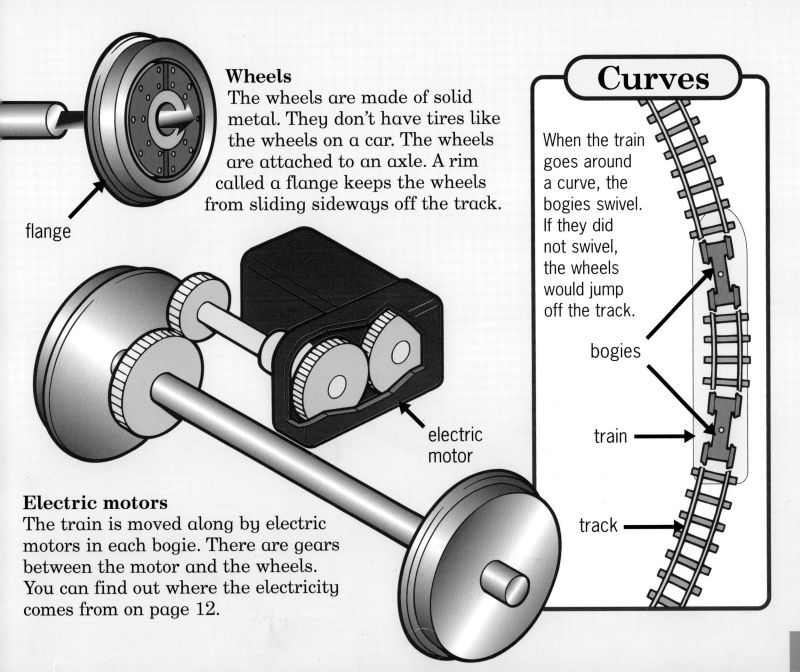

Wheels

The wheels are made of solid metal. They don't have tires like the wheels on a car. The wheels are attached to an axle. A rim called a flange keeps the wheels from sliding sideways off the track.

flange

electric motor

Electric motors

The train is moved along by electric motors in each bogie. There are gears between the motor and the wheels. You can find out where the electricity comes from on page 12.

Curves

When the train goes around a curve, the bogies swivel. If they did not swivel, the wheels would jump off the track.

bogies

train

track

The Track

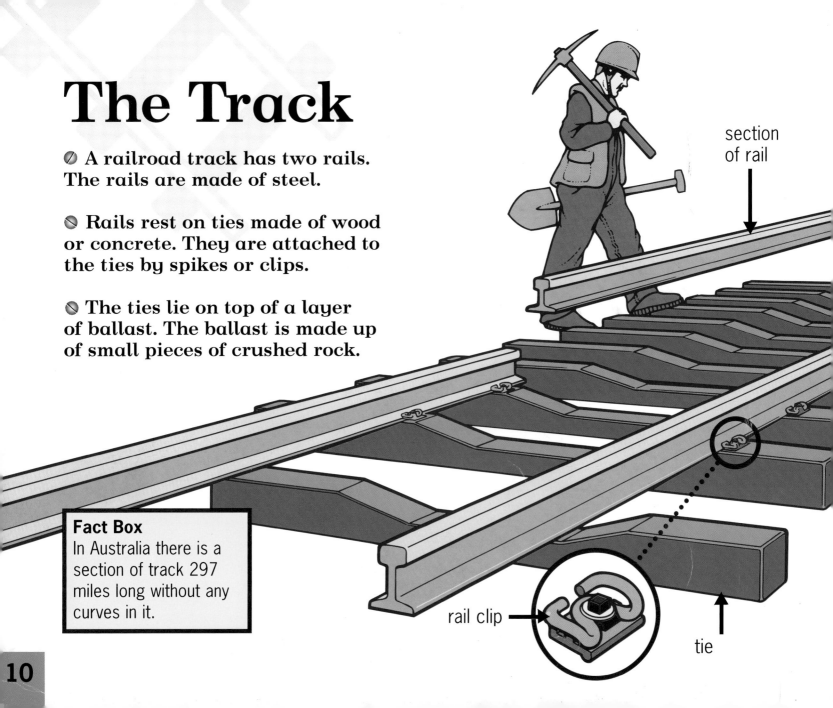

⊘ A railroad track has two rails. The rails are made of steel.

◐ Rails rest on ties made of wood or concrete. They are attached to the ties by spikes or clips.

◑ The ties lie on top of a layer of ballast. The ballast is made up of small pieces of crushed rock.

Fact Box
In Australia there is a section of track 297 miles long without any curves in it.

section of rail

rail clip

tie

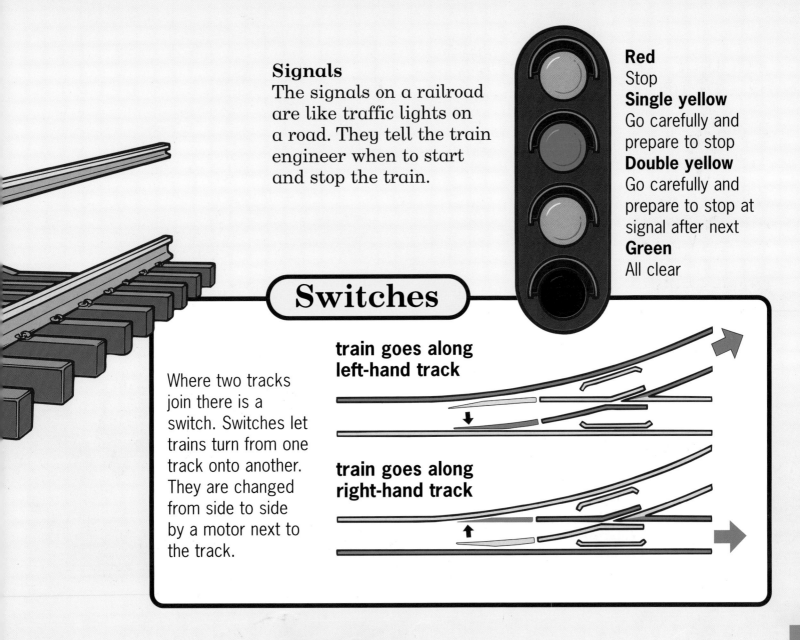

Signals

The signals on a railroad are like traffic lights on a road. They tell the train engineer when to start and stop the train.

Red
Stop
Single yellow
Go carefully and prepare to stop
Double yellow
Go carefully and prepare to stop at signal after next
Green
All clear

Switches

Where two tracks join there is a switch. Switches let trains turn from one track onto another. They are changed from side to side by a motor next to the track.

train goes along left-hand track

train goes along right-hand track

Getting Electricity

⊘ **The train in this book uses electricity to work.**

⊘ **The electricity comes from a cable above the track.**

⊘ **A pantograph on top of the power car collects electricity from the cable.**

⊘ **Inside the power car electric circuits carry electricity to the motors that move the train.**

Fact Box
The first electric railroad was opened in Brighton, England, in 1883. You can still ride on it today.

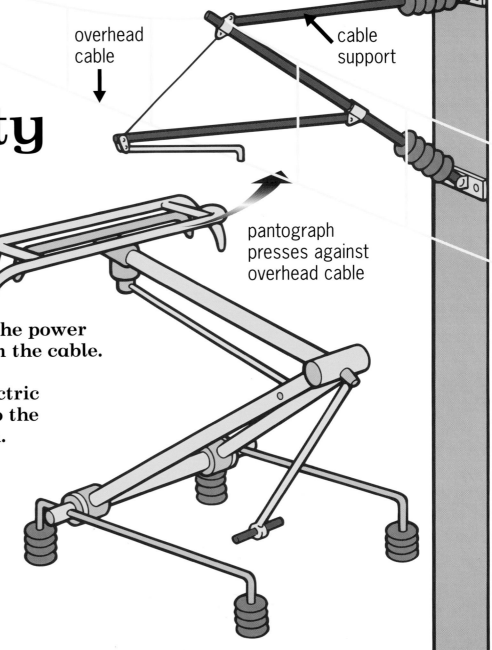

overhead cable

cable support

pantograph presses against overhead cable

Flow of electricity

Electricity from the pantograph goes to a transformer. Then it goes to circuits that feed the electricity to the traction motors.

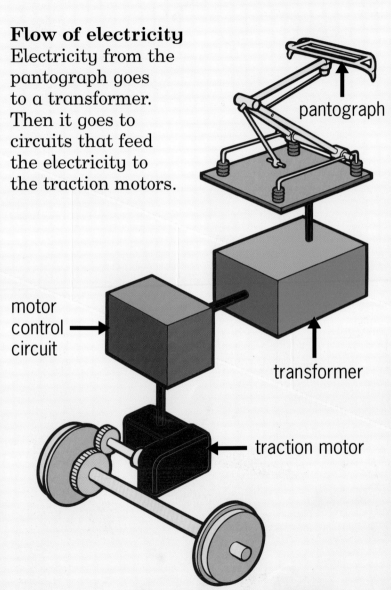

pantograph

transformer

motor control circuit

traction motor

The third rail

Some trains get electricity from a rail in the center of or beside the track instead of an overhead cable. This is called the third rail. A shoe slides along the rail to collect the electricity.

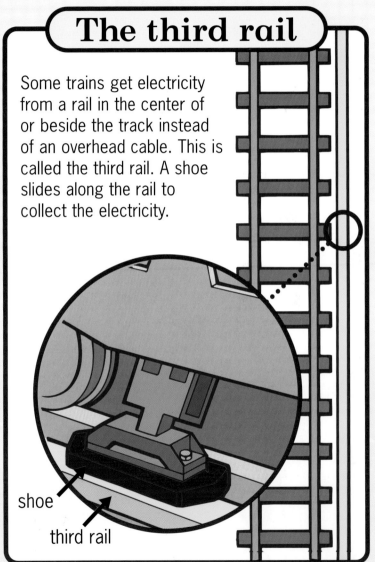

shoe

third rail

The Cab and Controls

 The engineer sits in a cab at the front of the train.

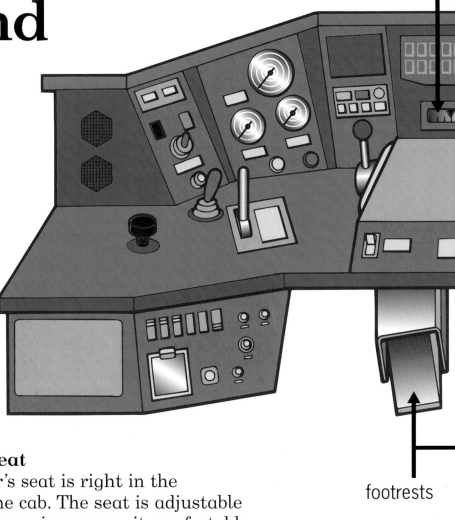 The engineer uses levers and switches to start and stop the train, to speed up, and slow down.

speed indicator

footrests

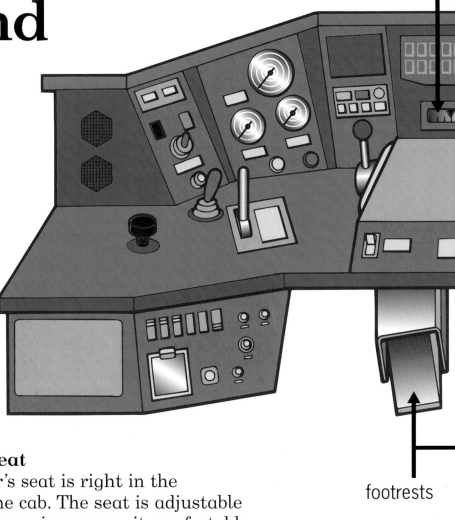 Lights and dials give information about the train, such as its speed.

Engineer's seat
The engineer's seat is right in the middle of the cab. The seat is adjustable so that the engineer can sit comfortably and reach the controls easily.

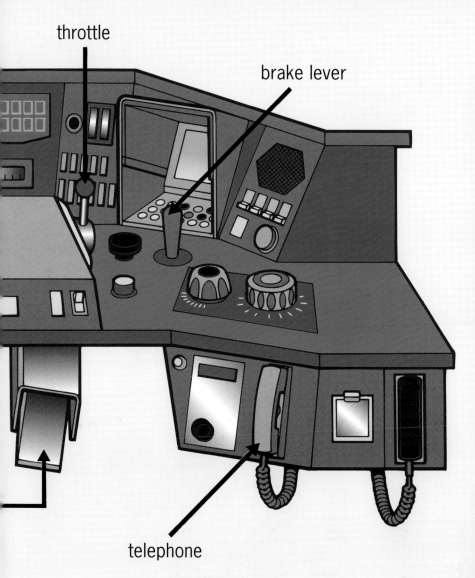

throttle

brake lever

telephone

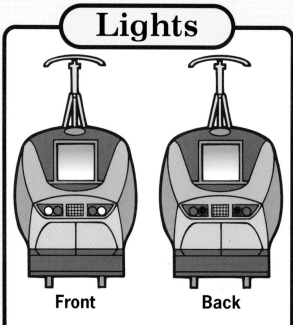

Lights

Front   **Back**

There are lights at both ends of the train. The lights are white at the front of the train and red at the back.

Fact Box
The engineer's throttle is sometimes called a dead man's handle. If the engineer lets go accidentally, the train stops automatically.

Passenger Cars

● Passenger cars have large windows to give the passengers a good view.

● Air conditioning keeps the cars warm in cold weather and cool in hot weather.

● The passengers can put their luggage on racks at the ends of the cars and above the seats.

Fact Box
On the first passenger trains, only first-class passengers had closed cars. Other passengers sat in open cars.

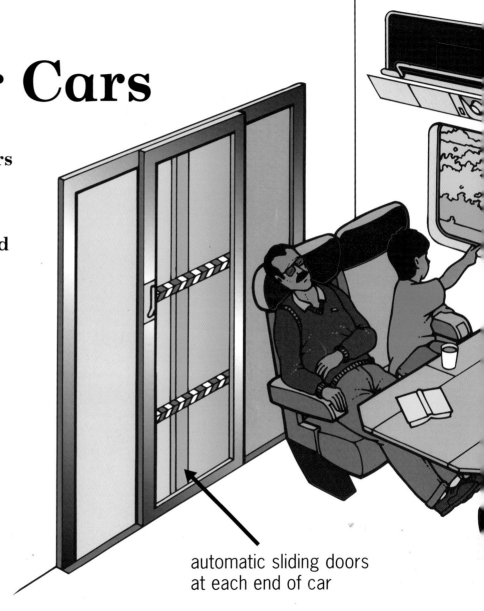

automatic sliding doors at each end of car

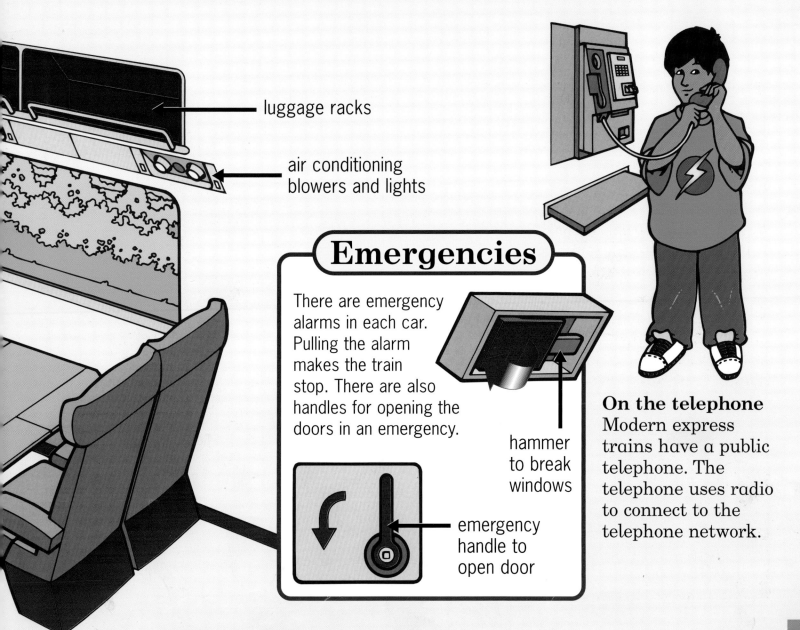

luggage racks

air conditioning
blowers and lights

Emergencies

There are emergency
alarms in each car.
Pulling the alarm
makes the train
stop. There are also
handles for opening the
doors in an emergency.

hammer
to break
windows

emergency
handle to
open door

On the telephone
Modern express
trains have a public
telephone. The
telephone uses radio
to connect to the
telephone network.

The Snack Car

menu

service counter

🔘 There is a snack bar in one of the train's cars where passengers can buy snacks and drinks.

🔘 The snack car has a kitchen where the food and drinks are prepared.

🔘 There are tables where people can stand to eat and drink.

Fact Box
You need lots of meals on the Trans-Siberian Express. It takes seven days to travel 5,778 miles from Moscow to a town called Vladivostock.

table

Hot food

The kitchen of the snack car has microwave ovens where food can be heated quickly. The kitchen also has water heaters for making hot drinks.

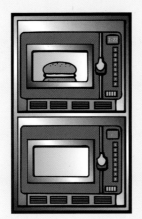

Snack-cart service

On some trains there is a snack cart as well as a snack car. The cart is wheeled through the train, serving snacks and drinks to the passengers in their seats.

Restrooms

At the end of each car there is a restroom with a toilet and sink. There are handles to hold on to when the train sways.

foot switch for flushing toilet

Carriers for Cars and Trucks

● Some trains carry cars and trucks instead of passengers.

● The cars and trucks are driven onto the carriers at the start of the journey and off again at the end.

These carriers carry cars through the Channel Tunnel between England and France.

doors between carriers open to let cars drive through

large door in carrier side

ramp to upper deck

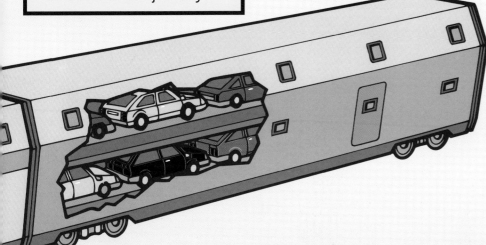

Flatcars

These special piggyback flatcars carry the trailers from trailer trucks. The truck drives the trailer on and off.

trailer on piggyback flatcar

trailer being unloaded

Car carrier

Carriers transport cars from factories to the showrooms where they are sold. The cars are tightly packed in and tied down to keep them from rolling.

Freight Cars

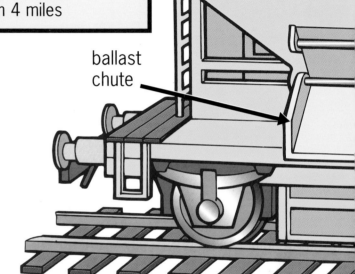

ballast
chute

💿 Freight trains pull cars carrying
different types of cargo, or freight.

💿 Some freight cars look like
boxes on wheels. The boxes are
filled with crates and packages.

💿 Some cars carry just one type of cargo.

💿 The cars have a coupling at each
end so they can be pulled in a long line.

Tank car
A tank car is a big tank on
wheels. It can be filled with
liquids such as oil or gasoline.
It has a ladder so that an
inspector can climb up and
look into the top of the tank.

Ballast car

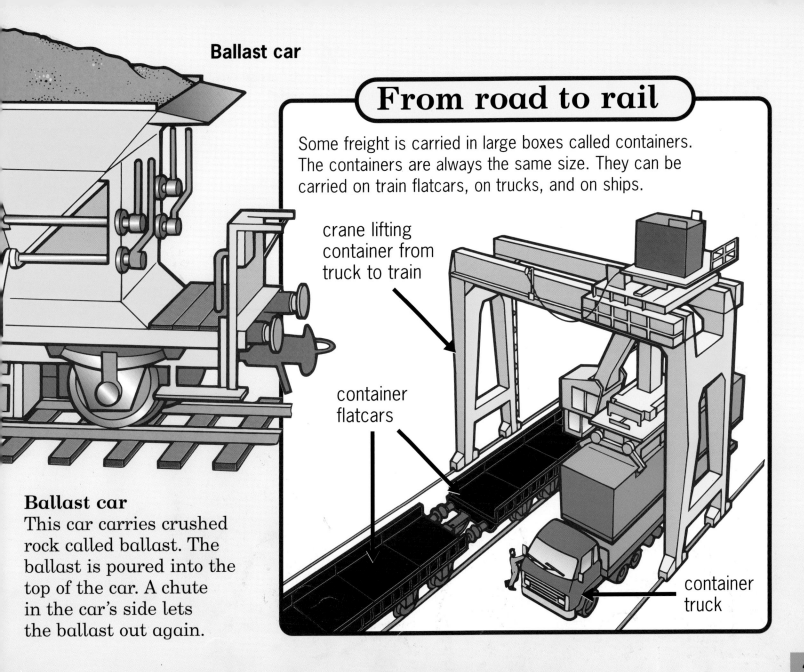

From road to rail

Some freight is carried in large boxes called containers. The containers are always the same size. They can be carried on train flatcars, on trucks, and on ships.

crane lifting container from truck to train

container flatcars

container truck

Ballast car
This car carries crushed rock called ballast. The ballast is poured into the top of the car. A chute in the car's side lets the ballast out again.

Diesel Locomotives

American diesel locomotive

- Some trains are pulled by a diesel locomotive.

- A diesel locomotive does not need electricity from power lines.

- It has a powerful diesel engine, which makes electricity for the locomotive's electric traction motors.

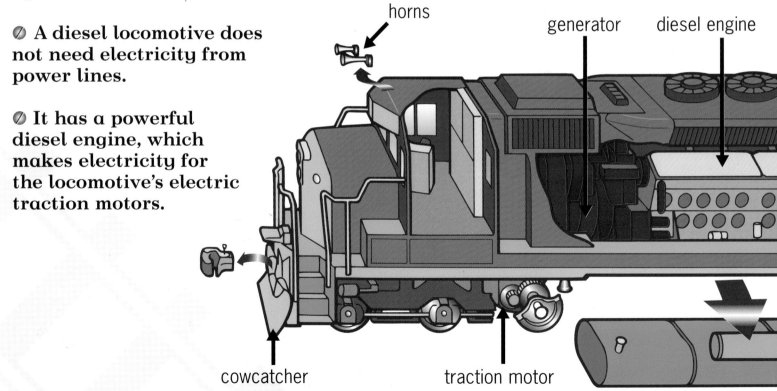

horns

generator

diesel engine

cowcatcher

traction motor

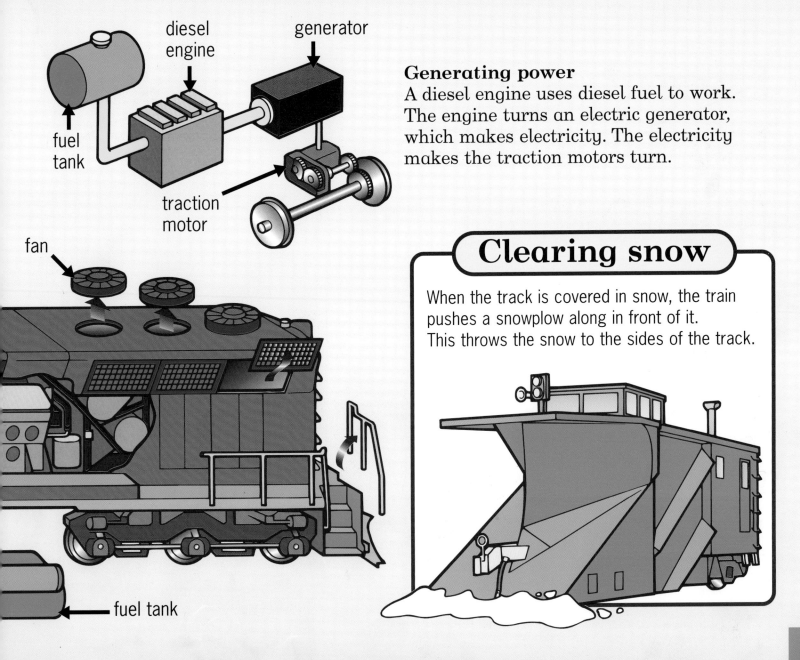

diesel
engine

generator

fuel
tank

traction
motor

fan

fuel tank

Generating power

A diesel engine uses diesel fuel to work.
The engine turns an electric generator,
which makes electricity. The electricity
makes the traction motors turn.

Clearing snow

When the track is covered in snow, the train
pushes a snowplow along in front of it.
This throws the snow to the sides of the track.

25

Special Tracks

◗ The trains on these pages travel on special tracks.

⊘ This is what trains and tracks might look like in the future.

⊘ Today there are only a few tracks like this in the world.

Monorail
A monorail track has only one rail. The train has wheels in the middle instead of at the sides. The monorail track is often built on tall pillars high in the air.

Monorail with train hanging underneath rail

Monorail with train on top of rail

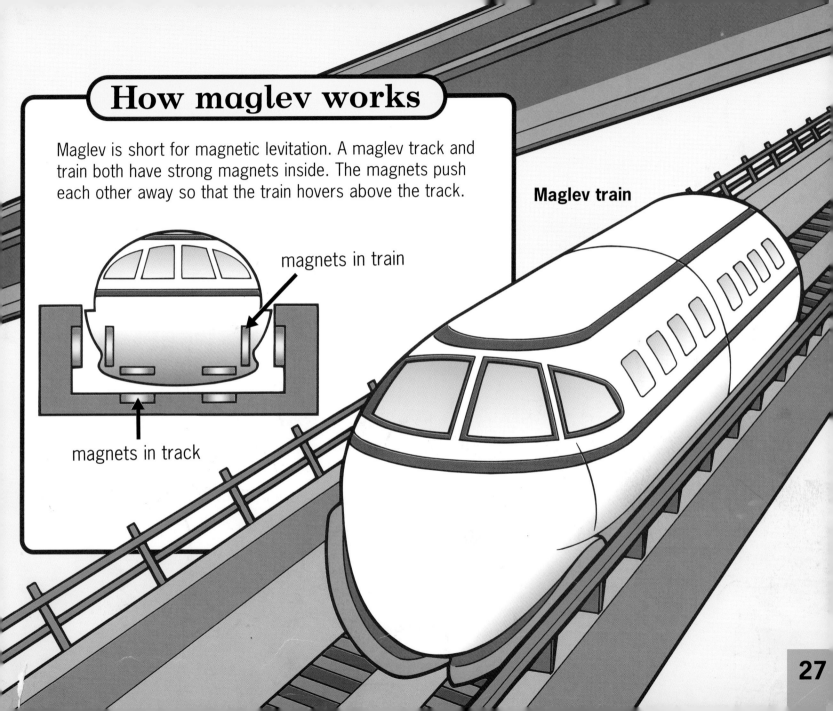

How maglev works

Maglev is short for magnetic levitation. A maglev track and train both have strong magnets inside. The magnets push each other away so that the train hovers above the track.

Maglev train

magnets in train

magnets in track

Underground Trains

- Some trains travel in tunnels under the ground.

- Many cities have underground trains because there is no room for tracks above ground.

- Stairs or escalators lead passengers down to station platforms deep under the ground.

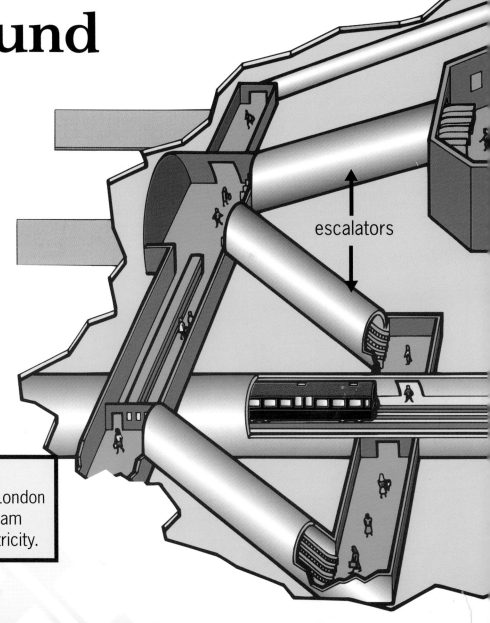

escalators

Fact Box
The first underground was opened in London in 1863. The trains were pulled by steam locomotives. Today they work by electricity.

street

ticket
window

platforms

NEXT TRAIN 2 MINS

When is the next train?
Each platform has signs telling passengers when the next train will arrive and where it is going. The signs are worked by a computer that knows where all the trains are.

On the map

Most underground railroads have many different tracks and lots of stations. Maps show how the stations are connected.

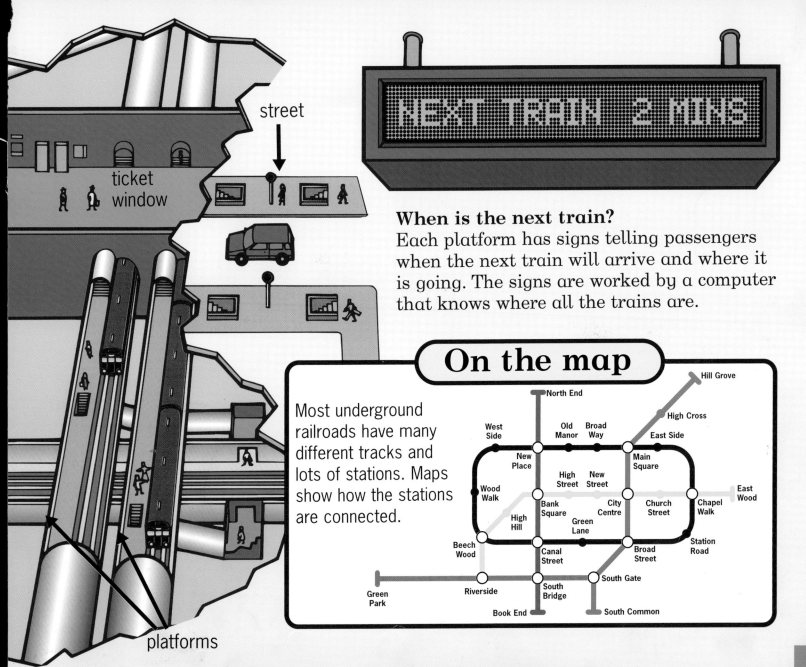

Hill Grove

North End

High Cross

West Side

Old Manor Broad Way

East Side

New Place

Main Square

Wood Walk

High Street New Street

East Wood

Bank Square

City Centre

Church Street

Chapel Walk

High Hill

Green Lane

Beech Wood

Canal Street

Broad Street

Station Road

Green Park

Riverside

South Bridge

South Gate

Book End

South Common

Useful Words

air conditioning A system that controls temperature and keeps the air fresh.

axle A metal rod that joins two wheels together. A train bogie has two or three axles.

ballast Small pieces of crushed rock.

bogie A frame with axles and wheels in it. Most power cars, locomotives, and train cars have a bogie at each end.

cab The space at the front of a train where the engineer sits.

cargo See freight.

diesel engine A type of engine that uses diesel fuel. Burning the fuel makes a shaft (a round rod) spin around. Most buses and trucks have diesel engines.

escalator A set of moving stairs powered by an electric motor.

express train A fast passenger train that connects large cities. It does not stop at small stations.

flange A lip around the rim of a train wheel that keeps the wheel from sliding off the rail.

freight Goods that are carried by cars on a freight train. These can be crates, packages, coal, oil, wood, or ballast.

gears A set of wheels with teeth around their rims. When two wheels are placed rim to rim, one wheel turns the other.

generator A machine that makes electricity when its shaft (a round rod) spins around.

levitation Hovering above the ground.

locomotive The part of a train that pulls it along.

pantograph The part of an electric train that collects electricity from the power lines that hang above the track.

power car The part of a passenger train that pulls the train along. Sometimes a power car looks like an ordinary car.

steel A type of metal made from iron, carbon, and often other metals.

suspension Springs that let a train's wheels move up and down over bumps in the track.

third rail An extra rail in the center of or beside the track that carries electricity. An electric train can get the electricity for its motors from the third rail.

throttle The lever an engineer uses to send power to a train's wheels. The engineer pushes the throttle forward to make the train go faster.

tie A concrete or wooden beam that rails rest on.

traction motor An electric motor that turns a train's wheels, making the train move along.

trailer truck A truck with a cab and a trailer that the cab pulls along.

transformer A machine that takes the electricity from overhead cables or a third rail and turns it into electricity that the traction motors can use.

ventilation grill A metal panel with holes in it that air can flow through.

Index

air conditioning
16-17
axle 8-9

ballast 10, 22-23
bogies 5, 8-9
brakes 15

cab 6-7, 14
cable 12-13
car carrier 20-21
clips 10
containers 23
controls 14-15
coupling 22
cowcatcher 24

diesel locomotive
24-25

doors 7, 16-17, 20

electrical equipment
5, 6, 9, 12-13
emergencies 17
engineer 6-7, 11,
14-15

fan 25
freight 22-23
freight cars 20-23
fuel tank 25

gears 9
generator 24-25

horn 24

lights 4, 14-15, 17
luggage racks 16-17

maglev 27
monorail 26

motors 9, 11, 12-13

panels 6-7
pantograph 5, 12-13
passengers 16,
18-21, 28, 29
passenger cars 6, 8,
16-19, 21
passenger train 4,
16-17
platform 28-29
power car 5, 6, 8, 12

rails 10, 13, 23, 26
restrooms 19

seats 14, 16
signals 11
snack car 18-19
speed 4, 6, 14
stations 28, 29
steam locomotive
8, 28

streamlining 4, 7
suspension 8
switches 11

tables 18
tank car 22
telephone 15, 17
TGV 4
third rail 13
throttle 15
ties 10
track 8-13, 25-28
traction motor 13, 24,
25
trolley 19
tunnels 20, 28

underground train 28

ventilation 6

wheels 5, 8-9, 22, 26
windows 4, 7, 16

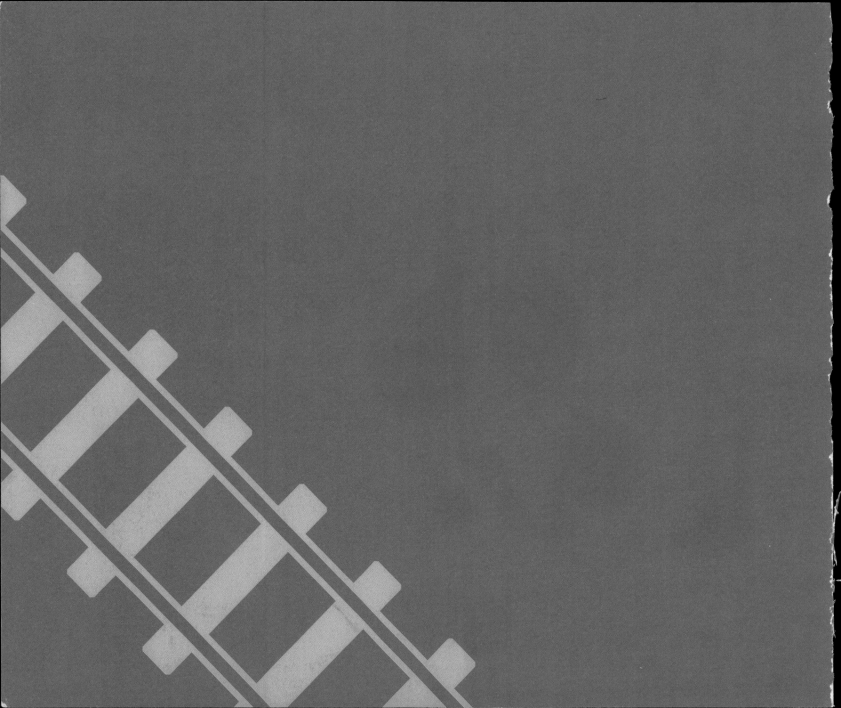